Parent's Introduction

Whether your child is a beginning reader, a reluctant reader, or an eager reader, this book offers a fun and easy way to encourage and help your child in reading.

Developed with reading education specialists, **We Both Read** books invite you and your child to take turns reading aloud. You read the left-hand pages of the book, and your child reads the right-hand pages—which have been written at one of six early reading levels. The result is a wonderful new reading experience and faster reading development!

You may find it helpful to read the entire book aloud yourself the first time, then invite your child to participate the second time. As you read, try to make the story come alive by reading with expression. This will help to model good fluency. It will also be helpful to stop at various points to discuss what you are reading. This will help increase your child's understanding of what is being read.

In some books, a few challenging words are introduced in the parent's text, distinguished with **bold** lettering. Pointing out and discussing these words can help to build your child's reading vocabulary. If your child is a beginning reader, it may be helpful to run a finger under the text as each of you reads. Please also notice that a "talking parent" ☺ icon precedes the parent's text, and a "talking child" ☺ icon precedes the child's text.

If your child struggles with a word, you can encourage "sounding it out," but keep in mind that not all words can be sounded out. Your child might pick up clues about a word from the picture, other words in the sentence, or any rhyming patterns. If your child struggles with a word for more than five seconds, it is usually best to simply say the word.

Most of all, remember to praise your child's efforts and keep the reading fun. After you have finished the book, ask a few questions and discuss what you have read together. Rereading this book multiple times may also be helpful for your child.

Try to keep the tips above in mind as you read together, but don't worry about doing everything right. Simply sharing the enjoyment of reading together will increase your child's reading skills and help to start your child off on a lifetime of reading enjoyment!

Habitats of the World

A We Both Read® Book: Level 1
Guided Reading: Level F

With special thanks to Brooke Wagner, Ph.D.
for her review of the information in this book

Use of photographs provided by Getty Images, iStock, and Dreamstime.
Text Copyright © 2017 by Sindy McKay
All rights reserved

We Both Read® is a trademark of Treasure Bay, Inc.

Published by Treasure Bay, Inc.
P.O. Box 119
Novato, CA 94948 USA

Printed in Malaysia

Library of Congress Control Number: 2016940078

ISBN: 978-1-60115-294-7

Visit us online at:
www.WeBothRead.com

PR-11-17

Habitats
of the
World

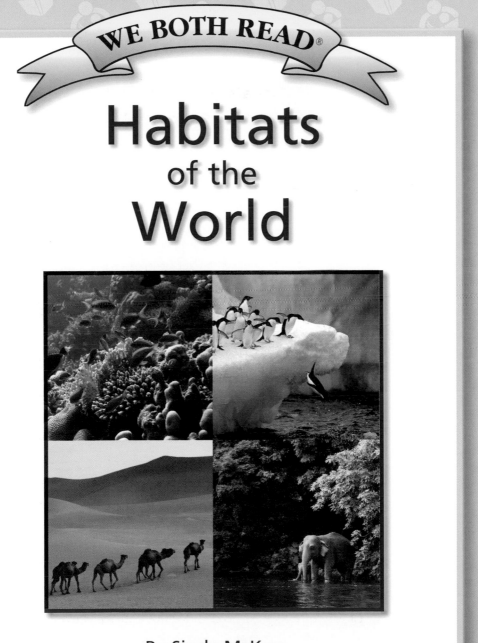

By Sindy McKay

TREASURE BAY

We live on an amazing planet called **Earth**. It is the only planet in our solar system that has liquid **water** and oxygen to breathe. It is the only planet we have found that can sustain **life**.

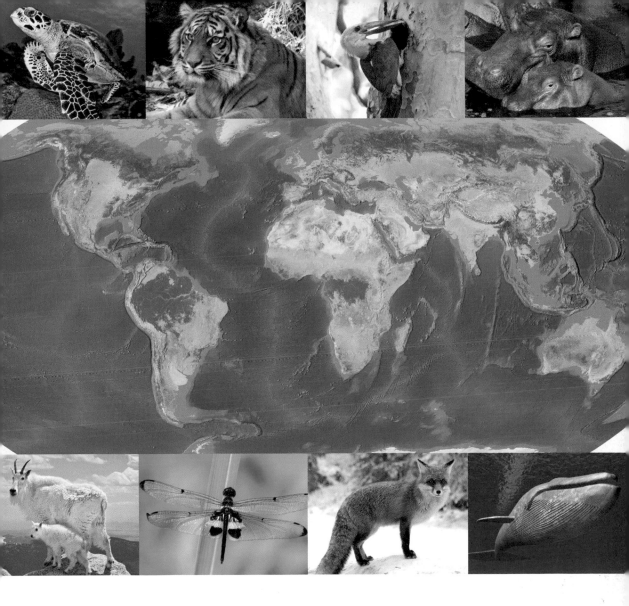

👁 This is a map of **Earth**.
There is **life** on land and
in the **water**.

Polar bears

Macaws

Alpaca

⊖ Earth has a huge variety of environments where animals can live. The place where an animal lives is called its *habitat.* A habitat provides the right water, food, and shelter for its native wildlife.

Some **habitats** are cold. Some are hot. Some habitats have a lot of water. Some do not.

The largest habitat on Earth is the **ocean**. The salty water of Earth's five **oceans** covers almost three-quarters of the planet. Just like on land, under the water are volcanoes, mountains, valleys, and plains. Many different kinds of sea **animals** live in this huge habitat.

Humpback whale

Goatfishes

Copperband
butterfly fish

Sea nettle jellyfish

Some **animals** in the **ocean** are big. Some are not. A lot are fish, but some are not.

Coral reefs provide a habitat near the shore, where the water is shallow and warm. The reefs sustain over a thousand types of colorful fish as well as dolphins, turtles, sharks, and rays. There are many different kinds of **corals**, and they are all living organisms that can grow and change.

Stony corals

Green sea turtle

Acroporida
stony cora

Soft corals and Caribbean reef shark

Various corals and purple tube sponge in foreground

Corals may look like plants,
but they are animals.

 Ocean water is salty. The rest of the water on Earth is called freshwater. Lakes are one kind of freshwater habitat. Many plants and animals, as well as many people, depend on the salt-free water of lakes to **live**.

Rainbow trout

Some animals **live** in the lake.
Some animals live on the banks.

River otters

11

Rivers provide another kind of freshwater habitat. Some animals live in or near the **river**, while others only go there to drink and cool themselves.

Hippopotamuses (hippos)

Grizzly bear

Bears get fish from the **river**.
Lions drink from the river.

Lioness and cubs

13

Wetlands, such as swamps and marshes and bogs, are habitats where shallow water covers the soil for a good part of the year. It is home to a variety of fish, reptiles, amphibians, mammals, insects, and **birds**.

Some **wetland birds** eat fish. Some wetland birds eat bugs. Some wetland birds eat fish *and* bugs!

Swamps have many trees growing in and around them. A mangrove swamp is especially rich in its variety of life. Mangrove trees have enormous roots that provide shelter for fish, birds, turtles, lizards, manatees, and alligators.

American alligator

Flame skimmer dragonfly

Mosquito

Firefly

There are lots of bugs and frogs in a **swamp**. The frogs eat the bugs.

Green tree frog

Polar bears

The polar regions are the coldest places on Earth. Much of the water is frozen in ice sheets and glaciers. Animals here have a thick layer of fat to keep them warm.

Harp seal pup

Antarctic fur seals

Chinstrap penguins

There are no plants on the ice,
so lots of the animals here eat fish.

The desert is a harsh habitat, where it can get very hot and there is very little water. The animals that live in the desert all need water to live.

When they find water, venomous Gila (HEE-luh) monsters drink as much as they can and store the water in **their** bladders to help them survive long, dry periods in the desert. Camels **store** water in **their** bloodstream.

Gila monster

Desert tortoise

Camels do not **store** water in **their** humps. The hump has a lot of fat. The fat is a way for camels to store food.

Dromedary camel

High mountain ranges are found all around the world. Native plants and animals must tolerate lower oxygen levels and extreme changes in temperature. The animals also must be good climbers! **Goats**, deer, and llamas have hooves especially designed for climbing.

Moose

Mountain goats

These **goats** have two big toes. Under the toes are soft pads. The pads help them to grip rocks.

While some animals live on mountains, others live inside them. Mountain **caves** provide a perfect habitat for many amphibians, spiders, insects, and some types of fish.

Mammals, such as raccoons and bears, may use **caves** to **sleep** in or for shelter in harsh weather.

Greater horseshoe bats

Persian trident bat

👀 **Caves** make good homes for bats. They like to **sleep** in caves.

White-tailed
deer

Deciduous (dih-SIJ-you-us) forests are especially beautiful in
the fall before the trees lose their leaves. Some animals, such
as deer and elk, live in this habitat all year long. Other animals,
such as birds and butterflies, migrate to warmer climates when
the weather turns cold. Bears stay in the forest and **hibernate**.

Grizzly bear and cub

Bears do not eat or drink when they **hibernate**. They wake up in the spring.

Barred owl

A coniferous **forest** contains mostly evergreen trees, such as pine and fir. In this habitat, the winters are long and the summers are cool. Large predators, such as bears, lynx, and wolves, can be found here. Many plant eaters also make this their home.

Lynx

Deer, elk, and moose eat the plants in the **forest**. The plants are on land and in the water.

Tropical rainforests sustain more than half of all species of plants and animals on Earth. Rainforests contain four layers of habitat—emergent, **canopy**, understory, and floor.

The emergent **layer** gets the most sun. Living here are **monkeys**, birds, butterflies, **lizards**, and bugs.

Sun conure parrots

Three-toed sloth

Parson's chameleon

🔵 Lots of animals live in the **canopy layer**. Birds, **monkeys**, and **lizards** are just some of them.

Spider monkey

Keel-billed toucan

The understory layer is the area beneath the leaves of the trees. It is made up of vines and other dense vegetation. Here you find more birds, butterflies, snakes, and frogs. Beneath the understory is the **forest floor.**

Giraffe beetle

Blue Morpho butterflies

Strawberry poison dart frog

Bengal tiger

Indian elephants

Mountain gorillas

The **forest floor** gets little sun. Here you will see tigers, gorillas, and elephants.

Grasslands provide a completely different habitat for animals, with open areas of grass and other low-growing plants. There are few trees or places to hide, so speed is important for the animals here.

The grasslands of North America are called **prairies**.

American bison (buffalo)

Black-tailed prairie dogs

👄 Skunks and **prairie** dogs
live here. Prairie dogs are
not dogs. But they do bark!

Giraffes

African grasslands are called **savannas**. Elephants, rhinos, and giraffes munch on the trees and grasses here.

Lions, cheetahs, and hyenas are some of the predators on the **savanna.** The predators prey on herds of animals, including giraffes and **zebras**.

African elephants

White rhinoceros and baby (calf)

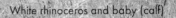 Animals on the **savanna** run a lot. **Lions** are fast, but **zebras** run faster.

Lions

Zebras

37

Life thrives in many different habitats on our planet. Unfortunately, many of these habitats are in danger. Pollution and cutting down forests can harm or destroy habitats. When this happens, it is hard for animals to **adapt** and survive.

Black bear

Some animals will **adapt**, but some will not.

Our world is full of beautiful and amazingly diverse plants and animals. It is our responsibility to preserve and protect this wondrous planet for future generations.

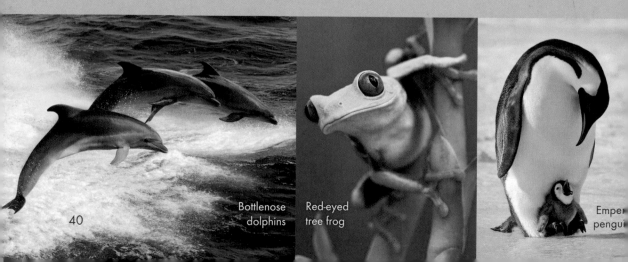

Bottlenose dolphins

Red-eyed tree frog

Emper pengu

It is up to all of us to take care of the Earth.

If you liked **Habitats of the World**, here is another
We Both Read® book you are sure to enjoy!

Amazing Eggs

Enter the fascinating world of eggs and hatch-
lings! Birds hatch from eggs, and so do reptiles,
amphibians, fish, and insects. Even dinosaurs
came from eggs! Learn about some of the most
amazing animals on the planet and how they
begin their lives—hatching from an egg.

To see all the We Both Read books that are available,
just go online to **www.webothread.com**.